SOCIAL MEDIA CAREER BUILDING™

20 GREAT
CAREER-BUILDING
ACTIVITIES USING
PINTEREST®

KRISTI LEW

ROSEN
PUBLISHING®

New York

Published in 2017 by The Rosen Publishing Group, Inc.
29 East 21st Street, New York, NY 10010

First Edition

Library of Congress Cataloging-in-Publication Data

Names: Lew, Kristi, author.
Title: 20 great career-building activities using Pinterest / Kristi Lew.
Other titles: Twenty great career-building activities using Pinterest
Description: First edition. | New York: Rosen Publishing, 2017. | Series: Social media career building | Includes bibliographical references and index.
Identifiers: LCCN 2016017427 | ISBN 9781508172703 (library bound)
Subjects: LCSH: Pinterest—Juvenile literature. | Online social net-works—Juvenile literature. | Career development—Juvenile literature.
Classification: LCC HM743.P56 L49 2017 | DDC 302.30285—dc23
LC record available at https://lccn.loc.gov/2016017427

Manufactured in China

Reference to and use of Pinterest does not imply endorsement or sponsorship, and our publication is for informational purposes only relative to possible uses of the Pinterest site.

CONTENTS

INTRODUCTION

Recipe

D o you enjoy connecting with people on Snapchat, Facebook, and Instagram? Then you may be interested in signing up for a Pinterest account, too. Like Snapchat and Instagram, Pinterest is a visually driven social network. However, Pinterest is a little different from the other social media platforms in that its designers never intended for it to become a social network. In fact, Ben Silbermann, the founder of Pinterest, told *Fortune* magazine that he views the site as a "catalog of ideas." His hope is to inspire people to collect thoughts, designs, and information that they will use to launch exciting new projects in the future. Despite his original expectations, however, connections are being made and Pinterest is rapidly becoming one of the top social networks on the internet.

The visually appealing, compulsively browsable site allows you to save images, videos, and infographics to themed pages, called boards. It is a great way to ignite individual creativity and to tap into the collective imagination of people with similar interests. It is also becoming more and more popular with schools, businesses, and employers.

The founder of Pinterest, Ben Silbermann, explains the website's potential to the media.

The name Pinterest is a combination of the words "pin" and "interest." Like an old-fashioned corkboard or refrigerator magnet, people use Pinterest to collect pictures and information they want to save for later. Unlike a messy old corkboard, however, these images come from all over the internet and are accessible anywhere that the internet is available. In addition, people far and wide can see and comment on the ideas others find compelling.

Each image, video, or infographic is called a pin. Pins link back to a webpage where more information can be found, making Pinterest a giant repository of knowledge, ideas, and inspiration. Because you can store, organize, and manage your own links as well as search other people's boards for related content, Pinterest is technically a social bookmarking site. Similar to a physical bookmark, pins save a specific place on the internet, allowing quick access to required information at a future date.

People who use Pinterest usually follow others with common interests. The pins of people you follow show up in your pin feed. A pin feed is a list of the pins from people, boards, and topics you follow. People who follow you will see your pins in their feeds, too. If you see a pin you like, you can bookmark the originating webpage by repinning it. You can also pin images, videos, and webpages directly from the internet. Or you can upload your own content to share projects you have completed or ideas you would like to try someday, possibly inspiring others to do the same. In this way, you can build and curate collections of webpages and concepts devoted to particular topics.

Pin collections are organized on themed boards. Boards resemble folders. They are intended to be spaces where you can collect similar ideas and related information. The result is comparable to having your own personally-designed catalog that holds all the wild, weird, and wonderful internet links related to your passions, hobbies, and aspirations. The activities in this resource can help you leverage the power of visual content to enrich your life, advance your studies, and promote your future endeavors.

CHAPTER ONE

Not (Just) a Pretty Picture

Pinterest is the brainchild of Ben Silbermann, who, with the help of his college buddy Paul Sciarra and a designer friend, Evan Sharp, began development of the website in 2009. Silbermann's objective was to build a platform that would enable creative people to showcase their individuality. The very first pin, posted by Silbermann himself, went live in January 2010. The site was first released, by invitation only, two months later. The founders purposefully limited the number of people who could sign up in the beginning. This limited registration allowed them to tweak the design and make it more user-friendly before the website was released to a wider audience.

A VIRTUAL STAR IS BORN

Two months after its limited release, with the help of a blogger named Victoria, who later became a Pinterest

Evan Sharp is the chief creative officer of Pinterest. He oversees all aspects of the website's design.

employee, Silbermann organized a "Pin It Forward" campaign to popularize the website. To Silbermann, targeting bloggers made sense because blogs, like the boards on Pinterest, are often devoted to a specific topic. The bloggers who participated in the "Pin It Forward" campaign were asked to make a board based on the theme of home. This activity proved to be popular and by August 2010, *Business Insider* reported

Millions of people use the Pin It button to bookmark useful websites, allowing them to return at a later date.

that the site had grown to around five thousand users. Over the following year, the site grew to millions of visits per week and was named one of the "50 Best Websites of 2011" by *Time* magazine.

A Pinterest iPhone app was released in March 2011, and the website grew again. A year later, the information services company Experian announced that based on the number of views, Pinterest had become the third-largest social media site behind Facebook and Twitter. By April 2012, the site had seventeen million users. Then, in August 2012, the invitation-only restriction was lifted. Now anyone could join Pinterest without an invitation. That same month, the company released an iPad version and an Android app. By September 2015, *Fortune* magazine reported that the company had reached one hundred million active users.

THE POPULARITY OF PINNING

The appearance of Pinterest in the social media landscape represented a seismic shift away from textual, chronological information to more visual,

> THE PRINCE OF PINNING

Ben Silbermann, cofounder and chief executive officer (CEO) of Pinterest, was born in 1982. He grew up in Des Moines, Iowa, where he attended Roosevelt High School. As a kid, Ben loved to collect things, especially insects and stamps. He was also intensely interested in technology and admired the work of Steve Jobs, Walt Disney, and George Eastman. However, Ben always assumed he would become a doctor. He had good reasons for thinking this—nearly everyone in his family was a doctor. Both of his parents, Jane Wang and Neil Silbermann, were ophthalmologists (eye doctors). Both of his sisters became doctors, too. Consequently, after graduating from high school, Silbermann entered Yale University as a premed student.

In his junior year of college, though, he had a change of heart. He graduated in 2003 with a degree in political science. The first internet search engines had appeared about eight years before, in the mid-1990s, and the internet was just becoming widely available when Silbermann graduated. After graduation, he was offered a job in the information technology (IT) department of a company in Washington, DC. This job reignited his boyhood interest in computers. He began to follow new businesses, such as Digg and Yelp, that were springing up on the internet and quickly decided that he wanted to develop a website, too. Silbermann also recognized that Silicon Valley would be a better place to realize his dream. So, without a job, he moved across the country to California.

Silbermann dreamed of working for Google, but he did not have a computer science or engineering background like most of the company's employees. Regardless, he applied for a position. To his surprise, Silbermann landed the job in 2006. This opportunity allowed him to learn more about a giant in the internet industry. He left Google in 2008 to start his own company, Cold Brew Labs.

Ben Silbermann admired what Larry Page (*left*) and Sergey Brin (*right*), the cofounders of Google, had created. Working for them gave Silbermann the desire to create his own innovative website.

collection-oriented content. Although the site originally was focused on collecting pictures, Silbermann and his partners soon turned their sights to connecting people and building a community and a culture instead.

In the beginning, many people did not see the need for another social media site. Silbermann combated this attitude by allowing people to integrate Pinterest content into their Facebook posts and Twitter feeds. Seeing interesting content in their friends' posts encouraged more people to check out Pinterest, even those who would not normally have visited.

Over time, Pinterest became known for certain genres of interest—primarily food, crafts, and fashion. However, as the site's popularity grew, businesses began to take an interest, too. Retailers quickly found that they could post pictures of new products and sales fliers. Pinterest users who were interested in a product pinned the item to one of their boards, which caused the pin to show up in the feeds of all of their followers. This spread of product information essentially increased "word-of-mouth" advertising for the company worldwide. Big businesses were not the only ones who benefitted from Pinterest's unique format. Small, start-up entrepreneurs quickly found ways to increase their client base, as well.

Today, Pinterest is used not only to pin pretty pictures but also for educational, creative, and professional purposes. With careful thought and curation, artists and students can create an

Recipe collections are popular on Pinterest. People use the search bar to find specific types of food or particular cooking methods.

online portfolio that can be used as a calling card for gallery proposals or college and job applications. Pinterest can serve as a positive promotional platform from which you can grow as an artist or as a person. Although beautiful pictures still drive Pinterest, its real purpose is to organize, plan, network, and connect. It can be considered a giant, communal collage that tells a story about the individuals, schools, and businesses that participate in the collection of worthwhile, interesting information.

CHAPTER TWO

Pin Like a Pro

To create a Pinterest presence that you can be proud of, you'll need to learn a few good techniques. Signing up for a Pinterest account is easy. Just go to the Pinterest website (www.pinterest.com) and enter your email or Facebook or Twitter account information. Use standard internet safety measures to protect your account. These measures include choosing a strong password and not sharing it with anyone, especially third party sites that want to pin things for you. Pinterest will only ask for your username and password when you log into the official website or application. Its employees will not call you or send you an email or a text asking for this information. If you receive such communication, it is likely a scam. Do not supply your log-in information to anyone, not even to friends.

BUILDING QUALITY BOARDS

Once you are signed up, you can change your profile. You do not have to fill in all of the information if you do

Create a strong password when signing up for Pinterest and protect it by not sharing it with anyone.

not wish to do so. However, you may want to change the default thumbtack icon to a picture. Other people tend to follow pinners with a profile picture more often than those who leave the default icon. Uploading a picture does not mean you have to upload a personal photograph. If you prefer, you can add a picture of something that interests you, such as a piece of artwork, a collection, or a design.

With an updated profile, it is time to start pinning. Before you begin, think about the type of image you want to project. What is your goal when using Pinterest? Are you using it to collect information for personal use or do you plan to use it professionally? Do you want your pins to be serious, smart, and thought provoking? Do you want to be seen as creative, clever, and entertaining? Try to come up with three to five words to describe your desired online presence. Keep those words in mind when designing your boards and choosing what to pin.

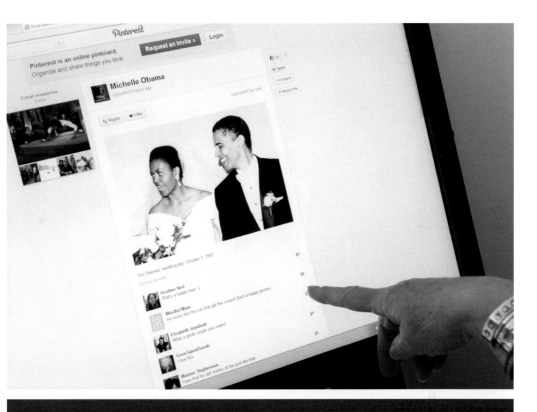

First Lady Michelle Obama uses Pinterest to share pictures of memorable events, such as her and President Obama's wedding day.

When you have decided on your goals and tone, you can start making boards. Click on your name and picture in the upper right-hand corner of the Pinterest website. On the left-hand side of the page, you will see a plus sign above the words "create a board." When you click on the plus sign, a dialogue box will open and you can fill in the name, description, and category of your board. These three pieces of information help people find boards they are interested in following.

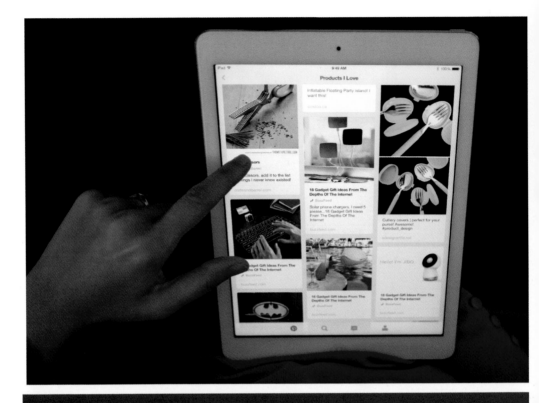

Pinterest is a great place to collect links to things that you are interested in buying, making, or sharing.

Your board names should be descriptive enough that people can tell what the pins on the board are about, but they should also be creative enough to catch people's attention. In the new board dialogue box, you will also have the option to make your board secret and to add collaborators. (Secret and collaborative boards will be discussed in Chapters 3 and 4.)

Now that your boards are set up, you will want to find the most visually appealing content to pin. You can locate this content in several ways. The fastest and easiest way to find subjects for your boards is to use the search bar at the top of your Pinterest page to search for things that interest you. When you find a picture you like, hover your cursor over the picture and three buttons will appear—a Pin It button, a Send It button, and a Heart button. Click on the Pin It button to pin the picture to your own board. The Send It button will allow you to share the pin with a friend on Pinterest, through your Facebook or Twitter feed, through Messenger, or by copying the website URL associated with the pin, which you can then send through email. Clicking on the Heart button will save the pin to your "likes." Liking a pin does not assign the pin to a particular board and it will not show up in your followers' feeds. Instead, it saves the image to a page on your profile. Using this option will allow you to sort your "likes" onto boards at a later time or delete them if you decide you do not want them.

Another way to find images and information for your boards is to search the internet. On some websites, you will find a red circle with an uppercase, cursive "P" in it. This icon is the Pin It button. Click on it and you will be given a choice of all the images on

The Pin It button makes it fast and easy to save the images you like.

that webpage. Choose the one you would like to pin and the board you want to pin it to. Sometimes, you will have a choice between identical pictures. If this is the case, choose the larger one. Larger images are often more eye-catching and are, therefore, repinned more often.

Not all websites have Pin It buttons on their images. For websites that do not, you will need to download a browser add-on called a Pinterest bookmarklet. Downloading this add-on will place a small Pin It button on your internet browser's toolbar. Having a Pin It button on your toolbar makes pinning content from the Web much easier. To get specific instructions on how to add the Pin It button to your browser, go to your profile page and click on the gear button. Choose "Get Help" from the drop-down menu and visit the Help Center. Under "Pinterest Basics," you will find a link to an article that will tell you how to add the Pinterest button to different browsers.

Finally, include a short description of each pin. Just a sentence or two is best. Many of the images you pin or repin will have a default description. Make sure the description actually describes what the pin is showing and that it fits your purpose and tone. You can edit pin descriptions when you pin them or you can come back to edit them later.

THE COPYRIGHT CODE

One of the most important aspects to remember when using Pinterest is to make sure you are respecting other people's copyright by giving credit where credit is due. Photographs and videos you have not personally taken must be credited to the original creator. The best way to accomplish this step is to make sure all of your pins link back to the original website or blog where the images can be found. Not only will this approach prevent you from violating copyright, but the whole idea behind Pinterest is to collect a body of knowledge that can be revisited at a later date. Pins that go to websites that are not related to the pin will prevent you and other Pinterest users from finding out more about the item pictured.

Website owners have the option of not allowing people to share images from their websites on Pinterest. If you try to pin something the owner of the image does not want you to, you will get an error message. Images with watermarks are generally not for sharing either. Respect the owner's wishes and do not try to sidestep this restriction by uploading the image yourself. Not only is this conduct disrespectful, it can also get you reported for copyright infringement. Reproducing copyrighted material, such as taking a photograph of pages in a magazine or a book, and uploading it as your own also violates copyright law. Pins that violate copyright may be reported and removed. If you consistently pin images improperly, your Pinterest account may be suspended and deleted. Repeat offenders may be permanently banned from the site. For any content for which you own the copyright, make it clear in the description that you are the photographer or videographer so questions of copyright infringement can be avoided.

WHO'S FOLLOWING ME?

People who use Pinterest follow boards or pinners with information they wish to collect. When creating a new board, think about the types of pins you want to go on it. Ideally, a board's topic will be broad enough to support several dozen pins but narrow enough that hundreds of pins will not apply. You can always move pins between boards if you create one that is too large. People are more likely to follow all your boards if you have around a dozen or so. Having hundreds of boards is more likely to lose followers than gain them.

If you already have followers, try not to pin dozens of images in rapid succession, especially if the images are similar. Keep in mind that your pins show up on your followers' feeds. If you pin thirty photos of cute cats in ten minutes, you may overwhelm your followers' feeds. No matter how much they like cute cats they may choose to unfollow you to get more variety. It is better to choose quality over quantity and to slowly build your boards over days or weeks.

After you have a collection of pins on a board, sort through them and choose the most compelling pin as the board's cover. When people visit your profile, a nice selection of board covers may entice them into following you.

Visit the boards of people who follow you. Follow them back if you like what they are pinning. You are not obligated to follow everyone that follows you, however. If you find someone that has some boards you like and others you do not, you can follow just those selected boards instead of all of their boards. Try to respond to as many neutral and positive comments as you can, too. By following these steps, you can build a community of people who share your common interests.

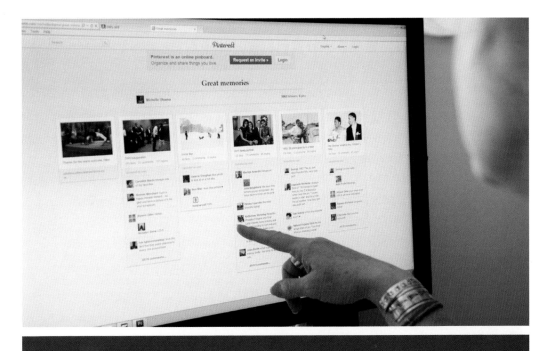

Think before you comment. Is your remark meaningful or mean? Is there any possibility of it coming across in a way you did not intend? If so, don't post it.

PROTECTING YOURSELF AND YOUR DIGITAL FOOTPRINT

Remember that everything you put on the internet is there to stay—potentially forever. Before you pin, think about how it will reflect on you. Will it foster a positive image or a negative one? If a college recruiter, a potential employer, or your grandmother googles your name, would you be proud of this board or would you want to hide it? If you want to hide it, don't put it up in the first place. Even if you delete a pin later, given

> DON'T FEED THE TROLLS

A troll is an internet bully. Trolls are people who say mean and hateful things because they think that no one knows who they are. The best way to handle internet trolls is to ignore them. Do not engage with them by commenting back. Many times, this lack of interest will cause them to go away. If they do not, take steps to block and report them. You can block someone by going to his or her profile, clicking on the icon that looks like a little gear, and choosing "block." You can find out how to report pins, comments, and messages in the Pinterest Help Center, too. If someone continues to bully you by making threatening remarks, posting photos you did not authorize, or by harassing or stalking you, ask a parent or other trusted adult for help. Cyberbullying is illegal. It may take some effort, but you can put a stop to it. Educate yourself about your rights so that you know what options you have.

the proper software, your digital trail can be followed. Do not post anything that may come back to haunt you.

Also, avoid sharing overly personal information. Always respect other people's privacy. Do not post pictures that have other people in them without their permission. Ask people who take pictures of you to do the same. In addition, when sharing your own photos, Pinterest will ask whether or not you want to share your location. If you are at home, you may not want to share your address for the whole world to see. Even if you are in a public space, think about whether or not you would want anyone and everyone on the internet to be able to find you. By the same token, if you are on vacation and post a group photo, sharing your location lets everyone know your house is empty. If you do not share your location when you post, no one can tell if the photo is current or if it is from a vacation you took in the past.

Not only are the images you share searchable, your comments are, too. Be nice in pin descriptions and when responding or leaving comments. If you would not say the same thing to the person's face, do not leave it in a comment. Ask yourself if someone—including law enforcement, your parents, and people you may someday want to work for—were to stumble across this comment, how will it affect his or her image of you? Use good judgment and create a digital footprint you can be proud of.

CHAPTER THREE

Neat As a Pin

Pinterest is a great place to create plans for future projects. You can find a wealth of inspiration for do-it-yourself (DIY) personal projects, from creating an awesome game room to making a list of all the places you want to visit someday.

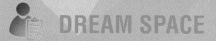 ## DREAM SPACE

Decorating is a popular topic on Pinterest, and ideas for pins are endless. If you can find your dream space pictured on a website, you can, of course, pin that to Pinterest, but why stop there when you can customize to your heart's content? You can also look for and find specific features. Want a climbing wall in your bedroom? How about a fairy portal to cover your electrical outlets? The directions on how to make or where to purchase those items and many, many more are out there. You can start with standard bedroom furniture and go on to paint colors, fancy sheets, book nooks,

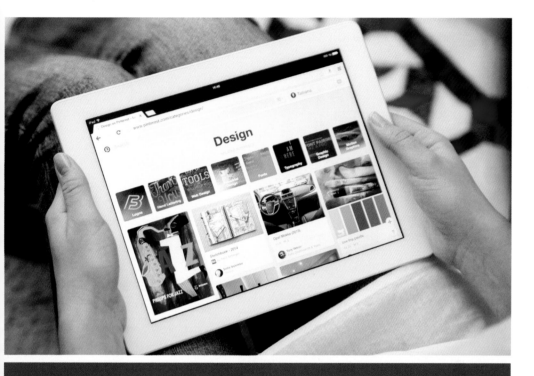

Gather ideas, design elements, and do-it-yourself tutorials to help you create a space that best reflects your style.

beanbags, and comfy floor cushions on which to lounge while reading or listening to your favorite music.

Your dream space may not be a bedroom at all. There are lots of ideas on how to create a space for your garage band to practice, outfit a home science lab, or perfect a video game or board game room. If you can dream it, you can find it. And, if you can find it, you can pin it. When you have a good idea of what you want your room to look like, tackle one project at a time until you make it a reality. Do not forget to upload pictures of your finished dream space. You might help others to build their dream room, too!

LEARN A HOBBY AND TEACH ONE, TOO

Are you interested in knitting, cooking, or stargazing? Or maybe learning a language or how to play a musical instrument is more your style. No matter what your hobby, Pinterest can help you tackle the learning process. Start a board devoted to the hobby you want to learn. Pin pictures of completed projects for inspiration. Search for and pin written and video tutorials and then work through them one by one until you master your chosen activity. Upload photos to keep track of your progress over time. Birdwatchers can catalogue the birds they have seen. Rock and insect collectors can keep records of their specimens and share knowledge

What are better than cupcakes? Cupcakes that won't go bad! Tips for faux cupcakes and other crafts are pinned and shared every day.

with other collectors. What if you're not sure of the identity of a bird, rock, or insect? Fellow collectors can probably help you out. Just upload an image and ask in the description. Once you have mastered your hobby, consider making tutorials to help others find joy in an activity you have some expertise in.

THINGS TO DO, PLACES TO SEE

What are some of the things you would like to do in your life? What do you want to be? You can use Pinterest to find inspiration and make vision boards that will motivate and inspire you to new heights. For example, you could start boards for all the places you want to travel. You can create a board for local places you wish to visit as well as one for the far-flung sights you want to see someday. Maybe you would like to create projects around some of these places, too. If you would like to visit Greece someday, for example, you might make a board that includes resources for learning how to speak Greek, several books about mythology and Greek history to read, or Greek or Mediterranean dishes you would like to sample or learn to cook.

You do not have to limit yourself to lifetime goals. Maybe you want to make a summer vacation vision board. You can make a simple list using a program such as Pinstamatic or you can find pictures that embody your vision and add descriptions that tell the story of what you want to do. Your summer vacation board may include going snorkeling and taking underwater pictures. Or maybe you want to go to the

Do you dream of traveling to exotic locations? Make a someday board to help you plan your trip. Even if you don't go right away, your board will keep you motivated to work toward your goal.

beach and join a beach volleyball game. Perhaps you want to learn a language, teach a child how to read, or volunteer at an animal shelter. Once you have your list, you can start working toward each goal, experiencing a fulfilling life and building memories.

CREATE A MEMORY BOOK

It can be fun to look back on the places you have been and the things you have done. There are many ways to use Pinterest to help you make a memory book. One way is to search Pinterest for scrapbooking ideas, save them, and then use them to make a physical scrapbook that you can keep. Another way is to create a digital scrapbook on your computer and upload your creations to Pinterest. Microsoft PowerPoint is one easy-to-use program that enables you to do this. Import your own photos, add clip art and decorations, and add music or videos if you would like and upload them to your boards. You can search for and follow scrapbookers on Pinterest for inspiration.

You can have one board for ideas, a board for specific events, like a birthday party, or boards that cover specific periods of your life, such as freshman year. If your boards start to get too big and you can no longer find what you are looking for, it might be time to separate ideas or events into smaller batches and make individual boards for them. If, for example, you begin following a lot of scrapbookers, you might want to have separate boards for layout ideas, embellishments, and themes.

You can share all or parts of your memory book with the Pinterest world or you can keep any or all of it private.

Whether you prefer keeping a physical scrapbook or a digital one, you can get interesting ideas and how-to articles on Pinterest.

You can share special moments with friends and family who could not be there by sharing the URL for the board with them, too.

SHOW OFF YOUR ARTISTIC SIDE

Pinterest is made for artistic self-expression. If you are artistic or crafty, you can make boards that showcase your artwork, fashion designs, or crafts. Not only will you have a record of all the pictures you have drawn, sweaters you have knitted, meals you have prepared, or outfits you have designed, but your great ideas can serve as inspiration for other people who are interested in the same pastimes.

If you eventually want to be an interior designer, you can start building your design talents in your spare time. Build boards with color ideas, sample rooms, interior layouts, and individual furnishings. Are you more interested in science or engineering? Make boards with pictures and instructions for building robots, rockets, catapults, zip lines, or any number of engineering projects. Learn to make beautiful crystal geode eggs, homemade lollipops, ice that glows in the dark, and crystal rainbows with the chemical know-how on Pinterest.

A BETTER YOU

Many people devote Pinterest boards to losing weight, healthy eating, and exercise plans. If you have similar goals, you may want to collect pins on these self-improvement projects as well. It is also a good place to pin quotes that motivate or inspire you to create a healthy lifestyle.

You can create boards with your favorite blogs, news sites, or online stores. If you visit these sites a lot, having them all in one place saves you time. You can also use your boards to pin good ideas or articles you do not want to forget.

Maybe your goal is to use social media effectively to support your personal or future professional goals. Search for boards on how to best use social media effectively. Are you stuck or are you procrastinating on your goals? Time management and productivity boards might contain the help that you need to get better grades and teach you how to use your time wisely so that you can fulfill all your dreams. Gather your materials and make a plan to reach your goals.

 ## STAY IN TOUCH WITH FRIENDS AND FAMILY

Do you have friends or family members who have moved away? You can keep in touch by connecting with them on Pinterest. Discover what they find interesting. Sharing engaging and relevant ideas with them can help you to still feel close to them. Perhaps you have a visit coming up. You could pin restaurants or places you want to visit together. You could also plan future trips together, events you want to attend together, or projects you want to do jointly. You could set up a group exercise plan and track your progress, choose books that you want to read at the same time, or plan a future party. You could set up a scavenger hunt in which each person has to find several items on a list and post a picture of that item. Any of these activities can help you feel close to someone and stay in touch with him or her frequently, even if that individual is physically far away.

THE FUNNY PAGES

Sometimes you need a lift. Pinterest can be a great diversion. Your Pinterest boards can entertain you, motivate you, and make you laugh. You can make

> A BOARD ALL YOUR OWN

When you create a new board, you will have the option to make the board secret. Secret boards can come in handy for events or lists you do not want everyone to see. Planning a surprise birthday party for your best friend? A secret board is a good way to go. Making a Christmas list for your friends and family is a good application, too. However, do use caution. Glitches happen. Do not pin something that would be embarrassing or compromising if it were accidentally revealed. You do not want to find distressing images out on the internet one day because Pinterest developed a bug during an update and your secret board is now public.

boards full of funny quotes, cartoons, and videos. Then, if you are feeling down, you will have a pick-me-up just a click away. There are many humorous boards on Pinterest that can be used for ideas and as a source of pins. Just remember that whatever you choose to pin reflects your personality and interests. Anyone can see what you find funny and choose to pin, so keep it tasteful.

CHAPTER FOUR

School of Thought

Pinterest is great not only for planning and organizing personal projects, but also for group projects. No matter what your group or committee is assigned to do, you can find inspiration on Pinterest and make an action plan there.

SCHOOL PROJECTS

Pinterest is an effective way to collaborate on school projects. Group members can share articles that relate to the topic and pin images of a prototype or a model you want to make. You can explore and save other students' projects that consider similar ideas as well as related real-world projects. Infographics, which are ways of showing statistics with simple, visual means such as graphs, lists, and pie charts, are very popular on Pinterest. You can use the site to research a topic and pin statistics to use later in a presentation (make

Are you working on a group project? Pinterest allows anyone in the group to collect the information they find on the internet so the whole group can use it.

sure you give credit to the originator or creator of the infographic).

There are also scores of science and art tutorials that may be helpful. Members of book clubs and literature classes can use boards to recommend books to one another, pin discussion questions for a particular book, or link to interviews with authors.

Use the description box to explain to other members of the group how the pin is relevant to your project. You can use the comments to discuss how you want to

PLURAL PINNING

You do not have to come up with all the ideas for a school project by yourself. By creating a board that other people can pin to, you can share and build on each other's ideas. You should always ask before adding someone to a group board. If you are working in a group, let the others in the group know that you will be setting up a board so that they know what to expect.

To set up a group board, you can either set up a new board or you can edit an existing board. When setting up a new board, you will see a box marked "Collaborators." The same box will appear if you edit an existing board. You can invite people to pin to the board by entering their email or their Pinterest usernames. This step will send the people an invitation. They will need to accept the invitation to pin to the board.

There are two other methods to make sure someone sees an idea you have pinned. One method is to tag the person in the pin description by adding the @ symbol in front of his or her username. The other method is to send the pin directly to the person. To do this, hover over the pin you want to send and click on the Send It button. Type the person's username or email address into the box that appears and hit the Enter key. A notification will appear in the person's email and on that individual's Pinterest page.

incorporate the pin's information into the project or to just bounce ideas off one another.

PLAN A PROM

Are you on the prom committee? Do you need some ideas for how to plan a magical, memorable event? Pinterest has some creative concepts. Searching for "prom themes" brings up a range of ideas—from "Under the Sea" to "Alice in Wonderland" to a 1920s theme. The search terms "prom decorations" or "party decorations" can give you plenty of ideas for DIY, inexpensive decorations. Set up a collaborative board so that everyone on the prom committee can add their ideas. Pin blog posts and websites with articles and DIY tips on how to make chalkboard signs, photo booths, and interactive games people can play between dances. Do not forget food and drinks! Pin recipes that fit your theme, too.

Once you have all your ideas, you can create a schedule that shows everyone who needs to do what job and by what date. Pin your schedule to your prom board so that the whole committee knows where to find it. Ask everyone to pin pictures of their completed tasks as well. People who are looking into places that can host your prom can pin pictures of ballrooms or other event spaces. Groups in charge of making decorations can pin pictures of their completed creations. Those designing announcements of the upcoming event can get ideas and pin their completed posters to Pinterest, too.

Are you planning a party or a prom? Pinterest opens up a whole world of ideas.

You will probably need to find a band or a DJ. If they have YouTube videos of their work, you can share them with the committee so you can all decide on who best fits the style of music you are interested in. You can also pin specific music tracks you that you can share with your chosen DJ. If your prom board is getting too big and unwieldy to find what you're looking for, you can separate pins into "Prom: Places," "Prom: Music," "Prom: Decorations," and so forth, to keep things more manageable.

ORGANIZE A SCHOOL TRIP

Planning a school trip can be easy and fun with Pinterest. You can save links for places to stay, restaurants to try, and museums, art galleries, or other points of interest to visit in the cities that you'll be traveling to. If you have a smartphone or other mobile device, you can access your pins on the go and your collection of activities will be at your fingertips during your trip. Gather information from tourism office sites, restaurant and attraction sites, websites, blogs, and newspaper articles that discuss the area. Popular review sites such as Yelp and TripAdvisor may be helpful. Do not forget to save maps of the city, bus or train schedules, and ticket prices. Once there, you can take photos of what you have done and what you have seen and add them to your board as a virtual scrapbook.

DIG THE DETAILS

Have you ever been in class and a teacher mentions an interesting idea but does not have time to discuss it in depth? You can use Pinterest to help you find compelling and informative articles online that pertain to the issues you're studying for school. This board can help make the subjects you are learning more fascinating, understandable, and relevant. Use your boards to make connections between what's being taught in the classroom and how the subject is used in people's lives and businesses. When you actively search out new and engaging ways to apply the things you are learning in school, you gain a better understanding of those topics and, as a result, your grades are likely to improve.

 ## MANAGE A MEETING OR PROMOTE A PERFORMANCE

You can use Pinterest to organize a meeting, conference, convention, seminar, or round-table discussion for an issue that you are passionate about. You can gather information about the issue, locate people who can speak about it, and spread the word. Share pictures of the meeting's venue and the people you have invited to make a presentation. Set up a link to books they have written and interviews that have been written about them. Design a flyer to entice people to come and pin that to your board. Make sure your pins link back to the conference website if you have one so that people can get more information.

You can also use Pinterest to promote a theatrical or musical performance. Link to the actors or musician's websites or to YouTube videos that show them in action. If you set up a group board, many people can add pictures and video to the board as the event takes place. If you want this occasion to become an annual event, you can direct people who might be interested in attending to the boards showing what has happened in years past. Being able to see what your event is all about could convince more people to come check it out.

Digital media can be a great way to help promote a live musical performance.

CATALYZE YOUR COLLEGE CAREER

How could Pinterest help you get ahead in college? Oh, there are so many ways. Even if you are just beginning to think about college, now is a good time to begin a college board. You can pin pictures and information about the colleges you are interested in attending. Investigate and collect facts about the towns they are located in. You can pin articles about principal courses

Pinterest boards can serve as a wish list or dream board as you investigate interesting colleges and majors.

of study, called majors, that appeal to you and follow experts in the fields that you are eager to pursue. You can bookmark internship and apprentice opportunities and find fascinating extra-curricular activities that you would like to investigate. Study tips, tricks on surviving your freshman year, and how to increase motivation and productivity might also come in handy.

CHAPTER FIVE

Pin It to Win It

Pinterest can be used to help find a job, support a cause, or build a business. Here are a few ways you can make money or further your career with Pinterest.

FIND A JOB

You can use Pinterest to give you a leg up in finding work. You can collect and organize information on the companies that you would like to work for, highlight your skills, show your expertise, and convey your personality. For example, imagine you are looking for a job in a restaurant or bakery. Assuming you are pursuing this line of work because you enjoy cooking or baking, you could pin images of meal presentations or attractive desserts you have made. Or maybe you are looking for a job as a carpenter or a welder. Videos demonstrating your woodworking or welding skills could be an asset in an interview. You could show off your video editing,

Do you dream of becoming a chef? Showcase your kitchen creations on Pinterest and share the link with restaurant managers and other prospective employers.

animation, or game designs as well. Pictures of school or charitable projects can help launch a discussion of your project management skills. Writers and journalists could link to online articles, book covers, or short stories to showcase their work. As the old adage goes: "A picture is worth a thousand words."

 ## SUPPORT A CAUSE

Because each pin is associated with a link, Pinterest can drive a lot of traffic to a website. Are you

› SEEING IS BELIEVING

Although some hiring managers still want to see a traditional, written résumé, others may be more open to a more creative form—the visual résumé. The type of résumé you will need will depend on what type of job you are applying for. It never hurts to have both at your disposal.

Before you begin creating your visual résumé, you'll need a plan. At this time, there is no way to rearrange pins on Pinterest. The pins are in chronological order, meaning that the pins you pin first are at the bottom of the board, while those you have pinned more recently are at the top. If you are trying to tell the story of your background—the schools you have attended, the companies you have worked for, organizations and charities you are involved with, awards you have received, and so on—you'll need to start at the end and work backward.

You can pin logos of schools and companies that link back to their web pages so recruiters can find more information about them. Pin photos of charity events you have participated in, videos that showcase your personality, and testimonials from past employees and colleagues. Use the description box below each image to explain how each pin relates to your career objectives or goals. Just in case the system that the human resources department of a company you are targeting can read only an old-fashioned résumé, make sure you put some time into that format as well. Then make a scan of it and pin that, too.

If you are passionate about animal welfare, consider using a Pinterest board to feature animals up for adoption at your local animal shelter.

passionate about the humane treatment and protection of animals? Or maybe your interests lie in environmentalism, finding a cure for a life-threatening disease, or wiping out homelessness, hunger, or poverty. Whatever the cause that drives you, you can use pins to help

raise awareness, educate others, and raise money to support that conviction. You can help educate other people about the issue by linking to articles, news stories, and charities associated with it. You can also meet other people who are just as passionate about animal rights, environmental issues, or other charities or nonprofits. You can repin their pins, make comments on them, and call people to action.

Pictures can be a very powerful way to raise awareness of causes and issues you care about. Visuals often create more visceral responses in people than do words. Because of these reactions, you'll want to steer clear of potentially upsetting or disturbing photographs. It is true that the more people feel, the more likely they will become interested in helping, begin to spread the word, and get involved themselves. However, you do not want to upset them. Most people on Pinterest are looking for beautiful, inspiring, positive images. Try really hard to keep the downers out of your feed. If you're interested in animal rights, for example, resist the urge to pin horrible pictures of abused animals. Instead, it is preferable to show rehabilitated animals and successful outcomes, such as a picture of the volunteers with all the animals they have taken care of. You can also share statistics, in the form of graphs or infographics, that may compel people to get involved. Do not forget to link to pages that tell people how they can donate money or volunteer.

BE YOUR OWN BOSS

Do you think you have what it takes to run your own business? Then you probably do. Get some tips on how to be your own boss by searching for "teen entrepreneur." You will find a long list of ideas, tips, and articles to help you along. Research ways to set up, maintain, and market your business by reading books, watching TED talks, and analyzing what the top pinners are doing. Let your images drive traffic to your Etsy page, your author page, or your website.

Think about ways you can set up boards to illustrate your focus. For example, if you make art from found items, such as hubcaps, empty tin cans, and other discarded materials, you could have a board that contains a picture of where each item in an art piece was found. You could add a time-lapse video showing the piece's creation or maybe one that shows what inspired the artwork. Finally, you could add a picture of the finished piece that links to a site where people can buy it.

BRAND YOUR BUSINESS

Branding your business helps build your audience. A brand is the way people see you and your products. For example, when you think of the technology company Apple, what words come to mind? For many people, those words are "hip," "fun," and "cutting-edge." Next, consider Apple's advertisements. Can you see how Apple's ads drive the way people think about its products? This process is called branding.

What should people expect when they visit your Pinterest boards and your website? Do you build robots or do you bake cupcakes? People interested in these two activities would have different expectations for website design and the information that is found on the site. Your pins should reflect that difference. Choose images carefully to create the proper tone and image for your business. The Pinterest account of an artist who sells nature-inspired jewelry should not look the same as one who sells handmade candy. One of the best ways to drive traffic to and from your website is by pinning the most appealing images that speak to your brand, whether it is colorful or sedate, cartoonlike or realistic.

MONEY IN THE MAKING

How can the fact that Pinterest drives traffic to websites help you earn money, even if you do not have something to sell? One way you can earn cash is to monetize your website through affiliate marketing. Suppose, for example, you have a passion for books and for reading. Maybe your website or blog is full of book reviews, upcoming releases, and information about your favorite authors. Appropriate pins to drive people to your site would include pictures of books, book lists, and author photos. To take advantage of affiliate marketing, you would choose an online store that sells books and book-related items and that offers affiliate marketing. The store you choose will have directions telling you how to add code to your website that will make a banner or box that people can click on to get to the store. Different stores have different rules dictating how affiliate marketers get paid. Some pay a commission if someone clicks from your website or blog to theirs and buys the item advertised on your site. Others will pay you a small fee if the person buys anything, regardless if it is the item shown on your site. Adding a Pin It button to your website should also be part of your plan. You want the people who have found your blog to be able to find it again. They can do so by pinning one of your posts.

Choose your affiliates carefully. If they do not relate directly to your Pinterest account and your blog posts, people who show up on your site will be disappointed. Not only will it be unlikely that they would click on the affiliate banner, but they may be so annoyed that they decide not to follow you any more. Be careful about the number of affiliate links you add to your site, too. Too many of them give your site a cluttered look and may make it download too slowly, which might cause people to lose interest.

THE POWER OF THE CROWD

Do you belong to a school group that has an amazing opportunity but doesn't have the money to take advantage of it? Crowdfunding may be a way to help finance your trip or event. Suppose your group has been invited to Italy to sing in an opera, for example. It would be a once-in-a-lifetime learning experience if you could just raise the funds for the group to go there. You could create a flier explaining how the trip would be beneficial and how people could help your group travel there. Pin pictures of your group singing in different performances. Pin images of Italian opera productions and information on their history and how they have affected world culture. Then ask people to donate to the group. Pin a fund-raising thermometer to your fund-raising board to show how much money you have raised so far and how much more you will need to make the trip happen. If you make your case compelling enough, hopefully, people will pin and re-pin your message, spreading it far and wide. Don't forget to link your pins to your website or your GoFundMe page.

School trips are not the only things that can be crowdfunded. Major creative projects, such as starting your own magazine, creating smartphone apps, or designing a video game, can be funded through Kickstarter. Use Pinterest to showcase your talents though pictures and videos, explain how people's donations could help you reach the next level, and link your pins back to your Kickstarter page. There is no telling where the power of the crowd might take you.

Organizing and curating your Pinterest boards can be entertaining and rewarding. Using them to plan and carry out projects can be even more fulfilling. If you find yourself spending more time pinning than doing, you may need to set up a schedule so you can do both. Use your "catalog of ideas" to create the life you want to lead and to become the person you want to be. Above all, have fun and keep pinning!

app An abbreviation of the word "application"; a software program.

block To prevent someone from interacting with you.

blog An online chronological log of thoughts about a particular subject or theme.

board A collection of related images and webpage links.

bookmarking To virtually mark a place on the internet for easy access at a later date.

branding To distinguish one business from another by tone and content.

browser A softward program used to display the World Wide Web.

chronological Arranged in order by date.

collaborative Made or produced by two or more people working together.

collage A collection of assorted objects and materials affixed to one surface.

copyright The legal right given to the creator of original artistic works to publish, sell, or distribute that work as desired and to protect the same work from being distributed by others without the creator's permission.

crowdfunding Raising money from a large number of people, usually through a website.

curate To deliberately select, organize, and assemble a body of work.

cyberbullying The act of threatening or harassing someone online.

digital footprint The traces and trails of activity online.

Etsy An online global marketplace.

feed A list of new content being added to a website.

GoFundMe A crowdfunding platform used by individuals for specific events or projects.

infographic A visual representation of data and text.

integrate To combine pieces into a whole.

Kickstarter A crowdfunding platform focused on funding creative endeavors.

pin An image, video, or infographic linked to a webpage where more information can be found.

profile The personal information and image a website user has chosen to share with the public.

re-pin To pin an image, video, or infographic found on Pinterest.

scam An attempt to get someone's personal information with the intention of using it for dishonest or illegal purposes.

social media Websites and applications that enable users to participate in social networking.

social network A website or application that allows users to interact and communcate with one another to share information, comments, and images.

TED Abbreviation for Technology, Entertainment, and Design, an organization that provides annual conferences and short video talks on a wide range of subjects.

troll A slang term for someone who intentionally starts arguments on the internet.

upload To transfer information from a personal computer or mobile device to the World Wide Web.

watermark A design that can be seen underneath text or overlaid on top of a picture or design.

FOR MORE INFORMATION

ORGANIZATIONS

Internet Crime Complaint Center (IC3)
National Press Office
Federal Bureau of Investigation
FVI Headquarters
935 Pennsylvania Avenue NW
Washington, DC 20535-0001
(202) 324-3691
Website: https://www.ic3.gov/default.aspx
IC3 is part of the Federal Bureau of Investigation (FBI).
The center's online complaint form can be used by
victims of online fraud, phishing scams, and other
internet crimes.

Internet Society
1775 Wiehe Avenue, Suite 201
Reston, VA 20190-5105
(703) 439-2120
Website: http://www.internetsociety.org
The Internet Society's website provides online tutorials
that explain what digital footprints are, how they can
cause problems, and how to manage your online
presence.

National Children's Advocacy Center (NCAC)
210 Pratt Avenue
Huntsville, AL 35801
(256) 533-5437
Website: http://www.nationalcac.org

The NCAC's website provides a list of online safety tips for kids and teens.

National Crime Prevention Council (NCPC)
1201 Connecticut Avenue NW, Suite 200
Washington, DC 20036
(202) 296-6272
Website: http://www.ncpc.org
NCPC's website contains resources that include a definition of and information about cyberbullying and how to prevent it.

Pinterest Corporate Offices
808 Brannan Street
San Franscisco, CA 94103
(650) 561-5407
Website: https://www.pinterest.com
Pinterest is a social bookmarking tool designed for discovering, saving, and organizing webpages that contain information about projects, ideas, and designs you want to access in the future.

PREVNet Administrative Centre
Queen's University
98 Barrie Street
Kingston, ON K7L 3N6
Canada
 (866) 372-2495
Website: http://www.prevnet.ca
PREVNet is a network of Canadian research scientists and youth-serving organizations devoted to the

understanding and prevention of all forms of bullying. Their website contains discussions about the impact of cyberbullying and the steps you can take to be safe online.

Royal Canadian Mounted Police Headquarters (RCMP)
Headquarters Building
73 Leikin Drive
Ottawa, ON K1A 0R2
Canada
(613) 993-7267
Website: http://www.rcmp-grc.gc.ca/en
The RCMP website includes an explanation of cyber-
bullying, its impacts, and what is considered illegal under Canadian law.

HOTLINES

Canada's Kid's Help Phone: (800) 668-6868
Cybertipline: (800) 843-5678
National Suicide Prevention Lifeline: (800) 273-8255

WEBSITES

Because of the changing nature of internet links, Rosen Publishing has developed an online list of websites related to the subject of this book. This site is updated regularly. Please use this link to access the list:

http://www.rosenlinks.com/SMCB/pin

FOR FURTHER READING

Christen, Carol, and Richard Nelson Bolles. *What Color Is Your Parachute? for Teens: Discover Yourself, Design Your Future, and Plan for Your Dream Job.* 3rd ed. Berkeley, CA: Ten Speed Press, 2015.

Criscito, Pat. *How to Write Better Résumés and Cover Letters.* 3rd ed. Hauppauge, NY: Barron's Educational Series, Inc., 2013.

Croce, Nicholas. *Enhancing Your Academic Digital Footprint* (Digital and Information Literacy). New York, NY: Rosen Publishing, 2013.

Grayson, Robert. *Managing Your Digital Footprint* (Digital and Information Literacy). New York, NY: Rosen Publishing, 2011.

Landau, Jennifer. *Cybercitizenship: Online Rights and Responsibilities* (Helpline, Teen Issues and Answers). New York, NY: Rosen Publishing, 2014.

Miller, Michael. *Selling Your Crafts Online: With Etsy, Ebay, and Pinterest.* Indianapolis, IN: Que, 2013.

Mooney, Carla. *Online Privacy and Social Media.* San Diego, CA: ReferencePoint Press, 2015.

Nakaya, Andrea C. *Internet and Social Media Addiction.* San Diego, CA: ReferencePoint Press, 2015.

Patchin, Justin W. *Words Wound: Delete Cyberbullying and Make Kindness Go Viral.* Minneapolis, MN: Free Spirit Publishing, 2013.

Rowell, Rebecca. *Social Media: Like It or Leave It.* North Mankato, MN: Compass Point Books, 2015.

Waters, Rosa. *Pinterest: How Ben Silbermann & Evan Sharp Changed the Way We Share What We Love.* Broomall, PA: Mason Crest, 2015.

Yearling, Tricia. *How Do I Keep My Privacy Online?* New York, NY: Enslow Publishing, 2016.

BIBLIOGRAPHY

Asghar, Rob. "Times Have Changed. Your Resume Needs to Change, Too." *Forbes*, May 20, 2013. (http://www.forbes.com/sites/robasghar/2013/05/20/times-have-changed-your-resume-needs-to-change-too-2/#47dc9f69583a.)

Booth, Angela. "7 Effective Ways to Make Money With Pinterest." Lifehack. Retrieved April 4, 2016 (http://www.lifehack.org/articles/money/7-effective-ways-make-money-with-pinterest.html).

Carlson, Nicholas. "Pinterest CEO: Here's How We Became the Web's Next Big Thing." *Business Insider*, April 24, 2012 (http://www.businessinsider.com/pinterest-founding-story-2012-4).

Carr, Kelby. *Pinterest for Dummies*. Hoboken, NJ: John Wiley & Sons, 2012.

Chandler, Stephanie. "Pinterest Power: How to Use the Third Largest Social Media Site to Promote Your Business." *Forbes*, June 13, 2002 (http://www.forbes.com/sites/work-in-progress/2012/06/13/pinterest-power-how-to-use-the-third-largest-social-media-site-to-promote-your-business/#6b35a48870eb).

Collamer, Nancy. "The 5 Ways Pinterest Can Boost Your Career." NextAvenue, June 7, 2013 (http://www.nextavenue.org/5-ways-pinterest-can-boost-your-career/).

Griffith, Erin. "Pinterest Hits 100 Million Users." *Fortune*, September 17, 2015 (http://fortune.com/2015/09/17/pinterest-hits-100-million-users/).

Jun, Paul. "Don't Feed the Haters: The Confessions of a Former Troll." 99U. Retrieved April 4, 2016 (http://99u.com/articles/25151/dont-feed-the-haters-the-confessions-of-a-former-troll).

Mansfield, Heather. *Mobile For Good: A How-To Fundraising Guide for Nonprofits.* New York, NY: McGraw-Hill, 2014.

Miles, Jason. *Pinterest Power: Market Your Business, Sell Your Product, and Build Your Brand On the World's Hottest Social Network.* New York, NY: McGraw-Hill, 2013.

Miller, Michael. *My Pinterest.* Indianapolis, IN: Que, 2012.

Morris, Heather. *Pinterest Kickstart.* New York, NY: McGraw-Hill, 2013.

Nusca, Andrew. "Pinterest CEO Ben Silbermann: We're Not a Social Network." *Fortune,* July 13, 2015 (http://fortune.com/2015/07/13/pinterest-ceo-ben-silbermann/).

Time. "50 Websites That Make the Web Great." Retrieved April 4, 2016 (http://content.time.com/time/specials/packages/article/0,28804,2087815_2088159_2088155,00.html).

Vimeo. "Ben Silbermann Keynote Address at Alt Summit." Retrieved April 4, 2016 (https://vimeo.com/user10165343/review/35759983/820bd84fa4).

Williams, John. "The Basics of Branding." *Entrepreneur.* Retrieved April 4, 2016 (http://www.entrepreneur.com/article/77408).

ABOUT THE AUTHOR

Kristi Lew is a professional K–12 educational writer and former high-school science teacher. She specializes in writing science textbooks, online courses, and nonfiction books for students and teachers. When she's not writing, she can often be found on Pinterest making lists of books to read, collecting recipes to try, researching ways to be more productive, or pinning geeky science humor.

PHOTO CREDITS

Cover Monkey Business Images/Shutterstock.com; p. 3 everything possible/Shutterstock.com; pp. 4–5 background solarseven/Shutterstock.com; pp. 4–5 (inset), 13 Josh Edelson/AFP/Getty Images; pp. 9, 12, 28 © AP Images; p. 10 © iStockphoto.com/zakokor; p. 16 Lewis Mulatero/Moment Mobile/Getty Images; pp. 17, 23 Saul Loeb/AFP/Getty Images; p. 18 Bloomberg/Getty Images; p. 19 Happy Zoe/Shutterstock.com; pp. 27, 46 Your Design/Shutterstock.com; p. 30 Pete/RooM/Getty Images; p. 31 Strakovskaya/Shutterstock.com; p. 37 Klaus Vedfelt/DigitalVision/Getty Images; p. 40 Moncherie/E+/Getty Images; p. 43 Tom Merton/Hoxton/Getty Images; p. 44 Images Bazaar/Getty Images; pp. 48–49 Camille Tokerud/The Image Bank/Getty Images; interior pages checklist icon D Line/Shutterstock.com; back cover background photo Rawpixel.com/Shutterstock.com.

Designer: Michael Moy; Editor: Kathy Kuhtz Campbell; Photo Researcher: Karen Huang